Baby Names

Baby Names for Boys and Girls, Baby Name Meanings, and Name Origins!

Table of Contents

Introduction

Thank you for taking the time to read this book: Baby Names. Also, congratulations on that fact that you're about to welcome a new addition to your family!

This book covers the topic of choosing a name for your child, and will provide you with a range of different names to choose from. Also provided are the meanings of each name so that you can choose a meaningful name for your son or daughter.

Picking the perfect name can be a stressful process for many parents. This book aims to make this process an enjoyable one by providing you with the best collection of names to choose from for both boys and girls!

This book includes the most popular names, unique names, famous names, alternative names, and many more! It will provide you with over 1000 different great names to choose from!

Once again, thanks for picking up this book, I hope you find it to be helpful!

Chapter 1:
Finding the Perfect Baby Name

The name is the first gift you will give to your bundle of joy, and picking the right name is almost certainly one of the most important decisions you can make before the big day arrives.

How to choose a name can be both a challenging and a stressful task for parents. A name that you feel comfortable saying and a name that your child will be proud of throughout his/her life are just few of the many considerations when choosing a name. With an overwhelming number of options to choose from, picking that perfect name for your child may seem difficult.

Whether you are looking for a unique name for your child or you want something meaningful, this book offers an excellent selection of baby names for boys and girls including their meanings.

Choosing a name is fun!

The process of pregnancy, getting everything ready for the big day, and deciding what you are going to name your baby can sometimes feel like a chore to fit in your already jam-packed schedule. So to make the task of choosing a name less stressful, the following are some ideas that you can try:

1. Jot down all the names you have in mind. You can also ask your family and friends to contribute a possible name for the baby.

2. Announce it. Tell all your friends and family members that you are looking for that perfect name for your baby

and that their suggestions would be very much appreciated.

3. Narrow down your choices. Pick at least five names that sound good when you say them. Write each one on a card and read them out every day for a week. You will see that at the end of the week, one will probably become your favorite.

4. Along with this book, you can leaf through magazines and even phone books to see if there are names that sound good to you.

5. Practice saying different names loudly and several times in a row. Then ask family members which ones they like best.

6. Read through the following names of boys and girls in this book, and note down your favorites!

Chapter 2:
It's a Boy!

The following are a list of names for boys, along with their meanings.

<u>A</u>

Aaron – meaning exalted, He is the older brother of Moses in the Bible who is appointed by God to be his brother's keeper. Famous people bearing this name include an American composer, politician, and singer. It can also be spelled in variations such as: Aharon, Aron, Aronne, Arron, Arrin, Aren.

Abba – Father

Abel – this means breathing spirit. In the Bible, Abel is the second son of Adam.

Abner – Father of light. Some of its variations include: Avner and Aviner.

Abraham – a wise man. Variations: Abe, Abrham, Avram, Abrahan, Avraham, Avrum.

Ace – meaning unity, one who excels.

Achilles – the Greek mythological hero who successfully fought with the Trojans. His ankle was the only part of him that could be injured, which explains why Science refers to that part of the anatomy as an Achilles' heel.

Adam – this name means man of the red earth. Adam is the name of the first man who made it into the world. This has been one of the most popular names in many countries and religions. Many parents pick this name for their first son. Some of variations include Adamh, Adamec, Addam, Adan, Addamson, Adams, and Addie.

Adolph – this is a German name meaning noble wolf. Some of the variations include Adolf, Adolfo, Adolphe.

Adonis – handsome

Adrian – a Latin word meaning black or dark

Afi – means fire

Ahmad – an Arabic word that means more deserving

Ahmed – Another Arabic word meaning praise

Aisea – meaning God saves

Akbar – A Hindu name meaning Muslim King

Alan – this means fair and handsome. Some of the variations include: Allen, Allan, Allayne, Allon, Alun, Allyn.

Albert – another common name for boys meaning brilliant. Some of the variations include: Albie, Alberto, and Albin.

Alden –wise, learned, old

Aldrich – an old and wise leader

Alexander - this is a Greek word meaning protector, defender, and helper of mankind. This name is considered to be one of the greatest and strongest names as it stands well on its own and there are many famous Alexanders in history such as Alexander the Great, and Alexander Haig, among others. Some variations include: Alec, Alejandro, Alex, Alistair, Alisander, Alsandare, Alexio, Alsandair, and Alexis.

Alfred – means wise listener

Allard – a French word meaning a noble one, brave

Altair – a Greek word meaning bird

Alvin – a German word meaning friend. This is a common choice of name for boys. Variations: Alvino, Alvan, Alvyn, Alvan, Alwynn, and Alvy.

Amadeus – One who loves God. Some of the variations include: Amadeo, Amado, Amahd.

Amir – powerful

Amory – leader

Andre – this is a French version of the name Andrew

Andrew – Brave. This is another common name for boys. This name conjures up both dignity and informality. Some of the variations include: Aindrea, Andres, Andi, Andrei, Andre, Andrey, and Andy.

Angelo – meaning messenger or angel

Anjay – a Hindu name meaning unconquerable

Anthony – a Latin word meaning valuable, praiseworthy. There are a huge list of famous people who bear the name Anthony like Anthony Perkins, Anthony Hopkins, Anthony Quinn, and a lot more.

Apollo – known to be one of the powerful Greek gods, this name means manly destroyer.

Arden – someone who is keen and eager

Argus – bright

Ariel – Lion of God. This can both be a name for a boy or girl. Some of the variations include Arel, Arielle, and Arie.

Armand – man on the army

Arthur – meaning rock

Arun – sun

<u>B</u>

Bailey- this is an English name meaning steward or bailiff

Balin – soldier

Barak – lightning

Bay – a Vietnamese word meaning born on Saturday

Beau – a French word meaning beautiful. Variation: Bo

Bello – assistant

Benaiah – meaning God builds.

Benedict – blessed

Benjamin – In the Bible, he was the youngest son of Jacob and his name translates to son of my right hand. Some of the variations include: Benje, Bennie, Benjimen, Benj, Benjamon, Ben.

Bentley – meadow

Berk – stable

Bernard – a German word for brave. Some of the variations include: Bernardo, Bernardion, Barnie, Bernie, Bernanrd.

Berwin – friend at harvest time

Bjorn – a Scandinavian word meaning bear

Blair – although most commonly given to girls, it can also be given to boys. This name means a flat piece of land. Some of the variations include Blayr, Blaire, Blayre.

Bliss – joy, happiness

Bob – famous, bright

Boris – warrior

Braden – meadow

Bradford – wide stream

Bradley – wide meadow

Bran – raven

Brandon – sword

Brent – mountaintop

Brian – Brave, virtuous

Brok – badger

Brody – second son

Bronson – dark man's son

Bruce - thick brush. Some of the variations include Brucio, Brucie, Brucey

Buddy – friend

Byron – cow barn

C

Caesar – hairy

Cain – spear

Caleb – brave

Calvin – bald

Cameron –river

Cappi – luck

Carl – or sometimes spelled as Karl is an English name meaning man

Carlos – a Spanish word meaning man

Cavan – good looking

Chad – protector, one who is strong

Chai - life

Cham – hot

Chi – an African word for God

Chiram – exalted brother

Chitto – Brave

Chonen – Gracious

Christian – the Anointed One. Some of the variations include: Christiano, Kris, Cris, Kristian.

Christopher – this is an English word meaning one who holds Christ in his heart. This name became popular among boys because there are a good number of famous Christophers such as St. Christopher, Christopher Plummer, and Christopher Columbus.

Clancy – son of a red-headed soldier

Clark – an English name meaning scholar

Clement – Gentle. Variations: Clem, Clemens, Celemento, Clemmie, Clemmy.

Clinton – town near a hill

Clyde – river in Scotland

Colby – dark farm

Colin – triumphant people. This name has become popular for boys, and to some extent also became a name for girls with variations including Cole, Coline, Collin, and Colyn.

Conan – elevated

Conrad – courageous adviser

Curtis – polite

D

Dakota – friend. This can also be a name for girls.

Dale – one who lives in a valley

Damian – this is a Greek word meaning tame. Some of the variations include: Damien, Damyen, Damienne, Damyon.

Dan – positive

Daniel – God is my judge. This name is Biblical in origin.

Daren – born at night

David – cherished

Dean – an English word meaning valet

Delvin – good friend

Demetrius – a Greek word meaning Lover of the Earth.

Dishon – walk upon

Divon – walk gently

Douglas – dark water. This is another common name for boys. Some of the variations include, Doug, Dogllass.

Drew – wise

Duncan – brown-skinned soldier

Dwight – blond

Dylan – son of the ocean

<u>E</u>

Earl – someone who is a noble man, leader.

Eden – delight

Edsel – home of a rich man

Egbert – bright sword

Elazar – God helps

Elliot – God on high

Elvin – old friend

Enzo – to win

Eric – ruler of the people

Ervin – beautiful

Esmond – rich protector

Ethan – from the Hebrew word meaning steady

Eugene – well born

Evan – God is good

Ezra – helper

F

Farr – wayfarer

Fawz – to accomplish

Feroz – lucky

Flint – stream

Floris – blossoming

Ford – river crossing

Frey – Supreme Lord

Frick – brave

Fritz – peaceful ruler

<u>G</u>

Gabriel – Man of God. This is a fully diverse name with significant number of names for parents to choose for their child. Some of the variations include: Gabi, Gabe, Gabby, Gabris, Gavi, Gavriel.

Gaius – rejoice

Galen – Healer

Galvin – sparrow

Gareth – gentle

Gerard – brave with a spear.

Germaine – one from Germany. Some of the variations include: Germane, Germayn, Jermaine, Jermane, Jermayne.

Gerywn – fair love

Gi – a Koran word meaning brave

Gil – joy

Gillean – servant of Saint John

Gino – living forever

Girvin – tough child

Godfrey – God is peace

Gomer – good fight

Grady – famous

It's a Boy!

Grant – great

Gyan – knowledge

<u>H</u>

Hadriel – God's glory

Hagan – home ruler

Hajj – an African word meaning born during the pilgrimage to Mecca.

Hale – healthy

Hali – sea

Halley – meadow

Hamish – a Scottish word meaning he who removes.

Hank – ruler of the state

Hannes – God is good

Hao – good

Hardeep – loves God

Harish – lord

Harper – hard player

Hasin – laughing

Hayden – hill of heather. This name is popular in Great Britain and Wayles.

Heman – faithful

Henley – high meadow

It's a Boy!

Herald – bearer of good news

Honore – honored one

Hulbert – shining grace

Hyo – a Korean word meaning childhood devotion

I

Ichiro – a Japanese word meaning first son

Ilias – the Lord is my God

Illtud – Lord of many people

Il-sung – a Korean word meaning superior, greater

Inokene – innocent

Ioela – God is Lord

Iona – dove

Irvin – beautiful

Isaac – laughter

Israel – struggle with God

Ives – yew wood

J

Jadon – God has heard

Jairus – God clarifies

Jal – wanderer

Jamar – newly created

Janesh – Lord of the people

Janus – born in January

Jared – a Hebrew word meaning descend

Jarell – new

Jaron – to shout

Jarvis – honorable

Jason – a Hebrew word meaning salvation

Javas – fast, speedy

Jazeps – God will increase

Jedrek – powerful and wealthy man

Jehu – the Lord is King

Jeremy – the Lord exalts

Jesse – God exists

Jethro – fame, popular

Jiro – second son in Japanese

Joah – God is his brother

Johar – Jewel

Jomei – light

Josha – satisfaction

Joshua – God is my salvation

Juri – farmer

K

Kacey – an English word meaning He announces peace.

Kahil – young

Kai – sea

Kaj – a Greek word meaning Earth.

Kala – black

Kalani – gallon

Kalea – Joy

Kaleo – one voice

Kaliq – artist

Kane – beautiful

Kaniel – a Hebrew word meaning reed

Kanu – beautiful

Kass – blackbird

Kay – joy

Keane – sharp

Keefe – beloved

Keiji – careful

Keith - forest

Kelii – wealthy

Kenn – brilliant water

Keoni – God is good

Khan – expected

Kiley – narrow land

Kim – gold

Kin – golden

Kirby – ray of light

Koji – a Japanese word meaning child

Korb – basket

Kosti – staff of God

Kukane – masculine

Kun – a Chinese word for Universe

Kyros – master

L

Lael – belongs to God

Laird – leader of the band

Lakshman – wealthy

Lambert- bright land

Lateef – gentle

Lazarus – God's help

Leighton – town by the meadow

Lenox – elm trees

Leonard – bold as a lion

Leroy – the king

Liang – a Chinese word meaning good

Llewelyn – lion-like

Lokni – raining through the roof

Lot – concealed

Lowell – young wolf

Lucas – this is considered as one of the popular names today meaning cool. It conveys a sense of intrigue and mystery

Lynch – mariner

Lynden – hill with lime trees

M

Maccrea – son of grace

Mackenzie – son of a wise leader

Maddox – generous

Maison – mighty warrior

Mafi – winner

Mahin – great

Makani – the wind

Malachi – messenger

Malcolm – a servant

Malkiah – God is King

Mamun – faithful

Mansur – divine assistance

Maoz – strength

Mori – my guide

Myron – aromatic oil

<u>N</u>

Naim – an Arabic word meaning happy

Naldo – good advice

Nam – south

Natin – a Hebrew word meaning Gift from God

Neil – champion

Nemo – smooth

Neto – earnest one

Nevin – holy. Variations include: Nev, Nevan, and Niven

Nigel – champion

Nimrod – a Hebrew word meaning rebel.

Noam – delight

Noe – quiet

Nola – little proud one

Nuri – light

O

Obasi – honoring God

Odell – forested hill

Odolf – wealthy

Ohin – chief

Oistin – respected

Olaf – forefather

Olery – leader

Omar – eloquent

Orion – son of fire or light

Orvin – friend with a spear

Osei – noble man

Oshea – helped by God

Oswin – divine friend

Oz – power

P

Patrick – noble man. Most Irish boys bear this popular name

Paz – peace

Penley – Fenced meadow

Penn – enclosure

Pepin – someone who perseveres

Perkin – little Peter

Peter – from the Biblical character meaning Rock.

Philo - loving

Pias – fun

Pin – faithful

Porter – gatekeeper

Pryor – leader of the monastery

Q

Quinn – wise

Quintto – home ruler

Quon – bright

<u>R</u>

Rabbi – my master

Rad – thunder

Radhi – goodwill

Radley – red meadow

Radman – joy

Ragner – power

Rand – fighter

Rankin – shield

Raphael – a Hebrew word meaning God has healed. Some of the variations include Rafael, Rafelo, Rafel, and Rafaello.

Rav – sun god

Ray – royal

Raza – content

Redley – red meadow

Redmond – counselor. Variations: Radmond, Radmund, Raymond, and Redmund.

Revee – bailiff

Regan – little king

Rene – reborn. Variations: Renne, Rennie, Renny, and Rennee

Renzo – laurel

Reyham – God's choice

Richard – a German word meaning strong ruler. Variations: Ricard, Ricardo, Richerd, Rick, Ricky, Richie, Ritch, Riki, Ritchy, and Ryszard.

Riley – brave

Rishon – first

Rocco – An Italian word meaning rest

Ronan – little seal

Roscoe – deer forest

Ross – cape

Roth – red

Rover – wanderer

Rozen – leader

Rye – strong ruler

Ryszard – a Polish word meaning brave ruler.

Sabir – patient

<u>S</u>

Sadler – saddle maker

Sagar – champion

Sahil – leader

Said – happy

Sancho – sacred

Sanjay – winner

Scott – one from Scotland. This is an All-American name and comes in variations such as Sot, Scottie for girls, Scotto, and Scotty.

Sean – God is good

Sef – an Egyptian word meaning yesterday.

Seif – sword of religion

Sen – wood sprite

Sepp – God will add

Serge – servant

Seth – to appoint

Sewell – strong at sea

Shafer – handsome

Shai - gift

Shamim – fragrant

Sharil – attractive

Shem – famous

Sherwin - bright friend

Shin – trust

Shiro – a Japanese word meaning fourth son

Simon – God hears

Sohan – charming

Stephen – crowned. This holds the distinction of the name of the first Christain on record. Some of the variations include Stefan, Stefanos, Steffen, Stephan, Stephanos, Steve, Steven, Stevie, and stenvenson

Strom – river

Sudas – good helper

Sudi – fortune

Sujay - successful victory

Sain – competent

Syon – happy

T

Tank – God of the sky

Tate – happy

Teo – gift from God

Theodore – a Greek word meaning Gift from God. Some of the variations include, Teodr, tedor, Teddie, Tedy, Teo Theo, Ted, and Tedd.

Tho – long life

Thor – thunder

Till – leader of the people

Tin- think

Tobbar – road

Tomer – tall

Torin – chief

Toru – ocean

Trent – rushing waters

Trevor – large homestead. Some of the variations include Trev, Trefor, Trvar, Trever, and Trevis.

Tory – solider

Todu – royal dynasty

Tyr – shining one

Tzuriel – God is my rock.

<u>U</u>

Ulric – wolf power

Ulrik – noble ruler

Urian – form the Greek word meaning Heaven

Ustin – just

Uziel – powerful

V

Valerian – healthy

Valin – mighty soldier

Vandan – salvation

Varen - superior

Vasin – leader

Victor – conqueror – this is considered to be one of the most popular names especially during the time of the Romans and sin Britain. Some of the variations include, Vic, Victoir, Victorino, Victirio, Vitoore, Vitto, Vitorio, and Vittorios.

Von – hope

W

Wail – one who returns to Allah

Waldo – strong

Walter – ruler of the people

Walwyn – Welsh friend'Wen – bron in winter

Wesh - forest

Wesley – western meadow

Whalley – forest by a hill

William – constant protector. Variations: Viliam, Vila, Vildo, Vilhelm, Will, Willie, Williamson, Willil, Willis, Willy, Willie, and Wilhelm.

Wynn – friend

<u>X</u>

Xavier – this is an English word meaning new house. Today, first names with an "x" are popular.

Xerxes – ruler

Ximen – Obedient

Xi-wang – a Chinese word for desire.

Xylon – lives in the forest

Y

Yair – God will teach

Yakez – heaven

Yana – He answers

Yardan – king

Yash – famous

Yen – calm

Yong – brave

Yosef – God increases

Yoshi – quiet

Yuan – round

Yuri – lily

Yushua – God's help

Yusuf – God will increase

Z

Zaccheus – pure

Zachariah – a Hebrew word meaning the Lord has remembered. Some of the variations include, Zacarias, Zach, Zachariah, Zeke, Zoko, Zakarios, Zako, and Zak.

Zaki – smart

Zale – strength of the sea

Zalman – peaceful

Zamiel – God has heard

Zamir - a song

Zane – God is good.

Zayn – beauty

Zake – the strength of God.

Zeki – smart

Zemariah – song

Zenas – generous

Zerach – light

Zeus – from the Greek word meaning King of the gods.

Zhu – a Chinese word meaning wish.

Zimran – sacred

Zindel – from the Hebrew word meaning protector of mankind.

Zion – guarded land

Ziya – light

Zomeir – from the Hebrew word meaning one who prunes trees

Zowie – life

Zuriel – the Lord is my rock

Zygmunt- victorious protection

Chapter 3:
It's a Girl!

In this chapter you will find some of the most popular girls names!

A

Abigail – From the Hebrew word meaning Father's joy. Some of the variations include: Abagail, Abegael, Abbey, Abbi, Abi, Abbigail, Abby, Abigale, and Avigail.

Abisha – a Hebrew word meaning God is my father

Accalia – a Latin word that is a mythological figure

Adalia – God is my protector

Adana – Father's daughter

Adara – noble

Adia – Gift from God

Adiva – gentle

Adora – much adored

Adriane – From the German word meaning Black Earth. Some of the variations include: Adriana, Adrianne, Adriannah, Adrien, Adreinah, and Adrienne.

Agatha – a Greek word meaning good

Agnes – virginal

Ai – From the Japanese word meaning love

Aiko – little one

Ain – an Arabic word meaning treasure

Aine – an Irish word meaning joyous

Airlea – fragile

Aiyana – to bloom forever

Aki – born in the fall

Akilah – smart

Alaia – virtuous

Alaine – rock

Alana – to float

Alberta – noble

Aldara – a winged gift

Aleen – bright light

Alei – leaf

Alesa – noble one

Alethea – truth. Some of the variations include: Aletea, Aleta, Alette, Alathea, Alithia, and Alithea.

Alexandra – this is a feminine version of the name Alexander. This means one who defends. Some of the variatons of this name include: Alexa, Alejandrina, Aleksy, Alexie, and Alexis.

Alice – noble

Alisa – happiness

Aliza – joyful

Alma – nurturing one

Alva – white, pure

Alya – to rise up

Amabel – lovable

Amica – close friend

Amira – leader

Amity – friendship

Amor – love

Amy – loved

Anastasia – resurrection

Andela – angel

Andrea – womanly. This is a feminine name version of Andrew.

Aneka – grace

Angela – messenger of God. Some of the variations include: angel, angelika,

Angele, Aangelie, Angeline, Angelita, Angie, and Anjelica.

Ani – a Hawaiian word meaning beautiful

Anina – answered prayer

Anisah – friendly

Anona – pineapple

Anthea – flower

Antoinette – priceless

Anya – grace of God

Arabella – in prayer

Aria – melody

Ariel – Lioness of God

Arlene – pledge

Artha – great wealth

Asha – desire

Ashley – an English word meaning Ash tree. This started out as a boy's name but

later on were given to girls as well. Some of the variations include: Ashlie, Ashly, Ash, Ashlee, and Ashton.

Atara – crown

Atrina – peaceful

Aura – slight breeze

Ava – birdlike

Avery – Elf advisor

Ayako – a Japanese word meaning damask

Ayumi – walk

Azaria – helped by God

Aziza – strong

Azua – beloved

B

Bambi – child. Some of the variations include: Bambie, Bamba, Bambina, and

Bamby.

Bariah – to succeed

Bathia – daughter of God

Bayo – an African word meaning happiness

Belia – oath to God

Bernice – she brings victory

Benita – God has blessed

Beryl – gemstone

Betuel – daughter of God

Bevin – singer

Bianca – white

Blaire – a flat piece of land

Blythe – happy

Bona – builder

Breana – strong

Brice – quick

Brina – defender

<u>C</u>

Cailin – triumphant people

Caitlin – pure

Calla – lily

Candra – radiant

Cara – Dear

Carissa – refined

Carla – meaning woman. This is a feminine version of the name Carl.

Casey – observant

Cassandra – protector

Cassidy – clever

Chalina – rose

Chantal – rocky area

Chanya – God's grace

Charis – grace

Charo – rose

Chasia – protected by God

Chazmin – flower

Cher – dear. Some of the variations include, Cherie, Cheris, Cherice, Sherry, Sherlyn, Sherilynne, Shery, and Sher.

Chesna – peaceful

Chiara – clear

Christine – anointed one. There are a number of famous Christine versions

Clementine – Gentle

Clytie – Splendid

Colleen – girl

Corrine – the hollow

Cyma – blossoming

Cyra – sun

Czarina – empress

<u>D</u>

Dada – curly hair

Dale – valley

Daniah – God's judgment

Danica – morning star

Danielle – God is my judge. This is a feminine version of the name Daniel. Some of the variations include: Denela, Denelle, Danice, Dannie, Danie, Daniella, Daika, Danylle, and Donita

Daphne – nymph

Dara – wisdom

Darda – pearl of wisdom

Daria – luxurious

Darlene – darling

Daryn – gift

Deanna – ocean lover

Deedee – cherished

Denae – innocent

Denise – lame god. This is the feminine version of the name ennis. Some of the variations include: Denice, Dennise, Dennie, Deny, and Denyce.

Deva – divine

Dianna – divine

Digna – valuable

Dinia – wisdom of God

Dinah – God will judge

Dorcas – Gazelle

Dorothy – gift from God

Drina - protector

E

Earlean – protector

Eda – happy

Eden – pleasure

Eilene – shining. This name is almost a given in girls of Irish heritage. Some of the variations include: Eilean, Ailene, Aileen, Alene, and Ilene.

Eira – Goddess of Medicine

Ela – intelligent woman

Eli – light

Elika – forever ruler

Elisha – God is my salvation

Elizabeth – pledge to God

Elsa – noble

Emily – industrious

Emma – embracing all

Enrica – leader

Erica- forever leader

Erna – capable

Eryl – observer

Ester – star

Ethel – noble

Eun – a Korean word meaning silver

Eustacia – fruitful

Evelyn – hazelnut

Faida – abundant

Farica – leader of peace

<u>F</u>

Fay – fairy

Felicia – happy. This is the feminine version of Felix. Some of its variations include: Felize, Feliz, Felicity, Falashia, Feliza, and Felicitas.

Fiala – violet

Filia – friendship

Frayda – happy

<u>G</u>

Gabrielle – heroine of God. This is the feminine version of the name Gabriel. Some of the variations include Gabbi, Gabby, Gabriella, Gabriele, and Gaby.

Gail – my father rejoices

Geela – joy

Gemma – jewel

Genesis – beginning

Georgia – farmer. This is the feminine version of the name George. Some of the variations include: Georgeanne, Georgeanna, Georgina, Gerogie, Georginne, Giorgia, amd Jorgina.

Gia – queen

Gianina – God is good

Giselle – oath

Glenda – holy and good

Godiva – gift from God

Gweneal – blessed angel

Gwyneth – happiness

H

Haidee – modest

Halia – remembering a loved one

Hana – flower

Harriet – leader of the house

Haya – from the Japanese word meaning fast

Heather – flower

Hebe – Goddess of youth

Heidi – noble

Helga – holy

Hilary – glad

Hilda – battle woman

Hiroko – a Japanese word meaning benevolent

Holly – plant

Honey – sweet

Hosanna – cry of prayer

Hye – a Korean word meaning graceful

I

Ida – youth

Ilka – admirer

Ilona – pretty

Ina – pure

Ingrid – beautiful

Irene – peace. This name has a rich history from the fourth century AD. Its popularity continued up until the middle of the fourteenth century.

Ishi – stone

Ismaela – God listens

Ivana – God is good

Iwa – A Japanese word meaning rock.

Izusa – white stone

J

Jacqueline – He who replaces. This is the feminine version of the name Jacob. Among its variations include, Jacalyn, Jacklain, Jackalyn, Jackalaine, Jackie,

Jacqualine, Jacqualene, Jacque, Jacqualyn, Jakelyn, and Jaquelyn.

Jaffa – beautiful

Janine – God is good

Jasmine – flower

Jaya – a Hindu word meaning victory

Jayne – victorious

Jemima – dove

Jena – patience

Jenelle – one who yields

Jennifer – this is one of those trendy names that became popular in the mid 70's and early 90's.

Jeremia – the Lord is great

Jillian – young. Some of the variations include: Jill, Jilliane, Julian, Juliane, Julliane, Gilli, Gillie, and Jillyan.

Jin – a Japanese word for excellent

Joan – God is good

Jolie – pretty

Josephine – a Hebrew word meaning God will add. This is the feminine version of the name Joseph. Some of the variations include: Jo, Josefa, Josefina, Josephina, Josie, Josi, and Josetta.

Jun – a Chinese word meaning truth of life

__K__

Kaisa – pure

Kal – yellow flower

Kalani – a Hawaiian word for heaven

Kalei – wreath of flowers

Kamea – sole one

Kameli – honey

Kamila – perfect

Kana – tiny

Kane – from the Japanese word meaning talented

Kara – dear

Karis – grace

Karmel – garden of grapes

Kasi – the holy city

Katherine – pure

Katriel – crowned by God

Kayla – pure

Kelly – female soldier

Kenda – magic

Kenzie – light one

Keren – animal horn

Kesia – favorite

Khalila – Good friend

Kichi – lucky

Kilia – heaven

Kimberly – King's meadow

Kira – throne

Kirsten – anointed

Kiyo – from the Japanese word meaning happy family

Korina – maiden

Kyla – crown

Kyra – lady

Kyrie – dark

L

Laine – bright one

Lala – tulip

Lana – rock

Lani – sky

Lara – famous

Larissa – happy

Lassie – young girl

Latifa – tender

Laura – laurel. This is one of those common names with different variations such as Laurette, Laurie, Loren, Lore, Loretta, Lori, Lorin, Lorinne, Lorie, Lorry, and

Loryn.

Lavinia – Roman woman

Leanna – flowering vine

Leena – devoted

Leigh – meadow

Leila – night

Leona – lion. The feminine version for Leon.

Letitia – happiness

Leviah – God's lioness

Lexa – man's protector

Lian – graceful

Lida – loved

Lila – dance of God

Linda – pretty one

Lisa – pledged to God

Lisandra – liberator

Loni – ready for battle

Luan – talk over

Lucy – light

Lulu – pearl

Luna – roman moon goddess

Lynn – pretty

M

Mabel – Lovable

Macia – defiant

Madai – to praise

Maeiko – a Japanese word meaning honest child

Maeve – delicate

Maha – big eyes

Mahira – quick

Maia – mother

Maisie – pearl

Makana – gift

Malia – defiance

Malu – peace

Manette – defiant

Mani – Buddhist prayer

Marabel – beautiful

Marcia – warlike

Margaret – pearl. Some of the variations for this name include: Maragarite, Margie, Margarette, Grettie, Gretel, Meg, Megan, Meggy, Meghann, Peggy, Reet, and Ritta

Margaux – champagne

Marian – combination of Mary and Ann.

Marigold – flower

Marini – healthy

Marni – to rejoice

Martha – lady

Mattea – Gift from God

Maxine – greatest is excellence this is the feminine version of the name Maximillian.

Maya – God's power

Mel – honey

Melia – yellow

Melissa – bee

Meryl – bright as the sea

Mina – From the Native American word meaning first daughter

Mia – mine

Michaela – a Hebrew word meaning who is like the Lord. This is the feminine version of the name Michael. Some of the variations include: Mikaela, Micaela, Mikail, Micki, Mikkie, Mickie, Mikella, Mikelle, and Mycheala.

Michelle – a French word meaning who is the Lord. This name has been on the top ten list of common names given to baby girls.

Mika – new moon

Miki – family tree

Mila – loved by the people

Milena – grace

Milica – hard-working

Millicent – born to power

Min – from the Chinese word meaning sensitive

Minda – wisdom

Mio – from the Japanese word meaning Triple cord.

Mira – rich

Mirella – God speaks

Misty – mist

Miya – temple

Mona – noble

Moray – great

Morgan – great and bright

Mori – From the Japanese word meaning forest

It's a Girl!

Mosi – first born

Mulan – Magnolia blossom

Muriel – bright as the sea

Myla – merciful

Myrtle – plant

<u>N</u>

Nadia – hope

Naeemah – generous

Naima – content

Nami – wave

Nancy – grace

Nani – beautiful

Nao – from the Japanese word meaning truthful

Nasya – miracle of God

Natasha – rebirth

Neima – powerful

Neola – young girl

Nerissa – sea nail

Neva – snow

Niamh – bright

Nike – Goddess of victory

Nina – girl

Nirel – cultivated pasture

Nixie – water nymph

Noelle – Christmas. Those babies born on Christmas Day are usually named Noel for boys or Noelle for girls. Some of the variations include: Noelene, Noella, ONoell, Noelene, Noeline, Nolekn, Noleen, and Nowell.

Nora – light

Nori – from the Japanese word ,eaning Principle

Norna – fate

Nuha – smart

Nydia – nest

Nyx – night

<u>O</u>

Odele – wealthy

Odelia – praise God

Odiya – song of God

Ola – protector of men

Olga – Holy

Olivia – Olive tree

Ona – grace

Ondrea – fierce woman

Oona – unity

Ora – prayer

Orela – revelation

Oriana – sunrise

Orya – peace

P

Page – intern, someone who commands power and respect

Paloma – dove

Panna – emerald

Patricia – noble. This is the feminine version of the name Patrick. Some of the variations include: Pat, Patreece, Patreice, Patrice, Patricia, Patricka, Patsy, Patti, Pattie, Trish, Tricia, and Trishia.

Paula – small. This is the feminine version of Paul.

Paz - gold

Peliah – God's miracle

Penda- beloved

Peony – flower

Phoebe – brilliant

Pixie – tiny

Prema – love

Priya – beloved

Pyrrha – red, fire

Q

Queen – queen

Quinn – advisor

Quintina – fifth

R

Rachel – lamb

Radha – prosperity

Rafa – well-being

Rafaela – God heals. This is the feminine version of the name Raphael. Some of the variations include: Rafa, Rafaella, Rafelia, Raffie, Rafaela, Raphaella, Raphella, and Rephaela.

Raisa – rose

Ramona – wise protector. This is the feminine version of the name Raymond.

Regina – queen

Ren – lotus

Renee – reborn

Reva – sacred river

Rhea – earth

Rhoda – rose

Ria – mouth of a river

Rida – content

Rima – antelope

Risa – laughter

Rita – pearl

Riva – joined

Rochelle – little rock

Ronni – strong counsel

Roselani – heavenly rose

Roxanne – dawn

Ruby – jewel

Ruchi – love

Ruri – Emerald

Ruth – companion

Ryba – fish

<u>S</u>

Sabbriya – patience

Sachi – Japanese word meaning bliss

Safi – fiend

Sakari – sweet one

Saki – cape

Salena – moon

Salida – happy

Salma – safe

Samantha – His name is God. This is the feminine version of the name Samuel. Some of the variations include: Sam, Saami, Sammie, Semantha, Siemantha, Simantha, and Symnathia.

Samara – protected by God

Samya – to rise up

Sancia – holy

Sanya – born on a Saturday

Sarah – Priceless

Sasha – protector of men

Sato – sugar

Saura – sun worshipper

Scarlett – red

Seema – treasure

Sela – princess

Selena – Goddess of the moon

Serena – serene, cute, mischievous

Sahina – gentle

Shaina – beautiful

Shamira – protector

Sharanee – guardian

Sharlene – woman

Shauna – God is good

Shawn – God is good. Another feminine version of the name John.

Sheela – gentle

Sheena – beautiful

Shera – light

Sheva – pledge

Shimona – to listen

Shina – loyal

Shirin – sweet

Shirley – bright meadow

Shomera – protect

Shona – God is good

Shyama – Dark beauty

Sidra – stars

Sigrid – beautiful victory

Silva – forest

Simone – God listens. This is the feminine version of Simon. Some of the variations include: simona, Simmone, Simonetta, Simonnette, Simona, and Symone.

Siti – Lady

Skyler – shelter

Solana – sunshine

Soma – moon

Sona – gold

Sonia – wisdom

Sophia – wisdom

Sora – songbird

Stacy – resurrection

Stella – star

Stephanie – crown. This is the feminne version of the name Stephen. Some of the variations include: Stefanie, Steffie, Stefanny, Staphaney, Steph, Stephny, Stephney, Stevana, Stevey, and Stevie.

Sukey –lily

Sulwen – bright sun

Sin-hi – A Korean word meaning loyal

Sunita – well-behaved

Suri – knife

Surya – Sun God

Sushanti – silence

Svea – kingdom

Syona – happy

T

Tabitha – gazelle

Taima – thunder

Tala – wolf

Talia – dew

Talise – beautiful

Talya – lamb

Tam – heart

Tamara – palm tree

Tamika – form the Japanese word meaning child of the people

Tansy – immortality

Tara – hill

Tasha – Christmas

Tasmine – twin

Tate – bubbly

Teresa – harvest

Tessa – beloved by God

Thana – thanksgiving

Thea – goddess

Thema – queen

Theodora – gift from God

Theone – godly

Thirza – pleasant

Tiara – crown

Tiffany – God's appearance

Tirion – gentle

Tish – happiness

Toby – God is good. This is the feminine version of the name Tobias. Some of the variations include: Tobee, Tobie, Thobe, Tobi, and Tobey.

Tomiko – A Japanese word meaning content child

Tora – tiger

Tracy – summer

Tricia – noble

Trixie – she brings happiness

Tzuriya – God is powerful

U

Udele – wealthy

Ula – jewel from the ocean

Ulria – wolf power

Urania – heavenly

Usha – dawn

Uta – A Japanese word meaning song

<u>V</u>

Vala – chosen one

Valerie – strong. This is considered to be one of the most popular names during the Roman empire. Some of the variations include: Valaree, Val, Valeree, Velery, Vallarie Valli, Valley, Vallie, and Vale.

Valora – brave

Vana – sea urchin

Vanessa – butterflies

Vanna – golden

Vashti – beautiful

Veda – wisdom, knowledge

Veera – string

Venus – love

Vera – faith

Veronica – true image. Some of the variations include: Veronique, Veronice, Veron, Verona, Verone, Veronika, Veroniqua, and Veronike.

Vica – life

Victoria – victory

Vida – beloved

It's a Girl!

Vita – life

Vondra – a woman's love

W

Waja – noble

Walda – ruler

Wanda – wanderer

Wanika – God is good

Welena – springtime

Whitney – white island

Wila – faith

Wilam – feminine version of William. Some of the variations include: Wilmina,

Wylma, Will, Wynette, and Wilmette

Winola – enchanting friend

Wyanet – beautiful

Wynn - fair, white

<u>X</u>

Xandra – protector

Xenia – hospitable

Xin – a Chinese word meaning beautiful and elegant

Xylia – forest

<u>Y</u>

Yara - honeycomb

Yakira – dear

Yamina – ethical

Yanaha – confronting an enemy, brave

Yashna – prayer

Yasmine – flower

Yasu – a Japanese word meaning calm

Yesenia – flower

Yeva – life

Yolanda – purple flower

Yonina – dove

Yori – Japanese word for honest

Yoshiko – quiet

Yovela – rejoicing

Yula – young

Yuriko – lily child

Yvette – arrow's bow

Yvonnne – Yew wood

Z

Zafina – triumphant

Zahra – blossom

Saira – princess

Zaira - princess

Zakiya - pure

Zara – dawn

Zarina – golden

Zaza – action

Zehara – light

Zemira – song

Zenda – holy

Zera – seeds

Serlinda – beautiful dawn

Zen – pure

Zhuo – a Chinese word meaning smart

Zinnia – flower

Zira – coliseum

Ziva – brilliant

Zoe – life. This is perhaps the most popular names for girls and have picked up the steam since the stat of the 90's. Some of the variations include: Zoey and Zoie.

Zora – dawn

Zorina – golden

Zuri – beautiful

Zuzana – rose

Chapter 4:
The 200 Most Popular Boy's Names

This chapter includes the top 200 most popular boy's names in the year 2016.

1. Liam
2. Noah
3. Ethan
4. Mason
5. Lucas
6. Logan
7. Oliver
8. Jackson
9. Aiden
10. Jacob
11. Elijah
12. James
13. Benjamin
14. Alexander
15. Jack

16. Luke

17. William

18. Carter

19. Michael

20. Daniel

21. Owen

22. Gabriel

23. Henry

24. Matthew

25. Wyatt

26. Jayden

27. Nathan

28. Isaac

29. Ryan

30. Caleb

31. Sebastian

32. David

33. Andrew

34. Dylan

35. Samuel

36. Connor

37. Jaxon

38. Joshua

39. Eli

40. Hunter

41. Grayson

42. Landon

43. Levi

44. Julian

45. Anthony

46. Joseph

47. Max

48. John

49. Adam

50. Christian

51. Cameron

52. Leo

53. Gavin

54. Lincoln

55. Isaiah

56. Evan

57. Nolan

58. Thomas

59. Dominic

60. Hudson

61. Muhammad

62. Brayden

63. Christopher

64. Aaron

65. Parker

66. Colton

67. Nicholas

68. Austin

69. Adrian

70. Charlie

71. Josiah

72. Cooper

73. Tyler

74. Jonathan

75. Chase

76. Jordan

77. Asher

78. Jeremiah

79. Jace

80. Jaxson

81. Ian

82. Alex

83. Easton

84. Zachary

85. Ezra

86. Carson

87. Miles

88. Xavier

89. Declan

90. Ayden

91. Blake

92. Tristan

93. Cole

94. Nathaniel

95. Ryder

96. Micah

97. Jason

98. Harrison

99. Sawyer

100. Mateo

101. Brody

102. Camden

103. Greyson

104. Roman

105. Elias

106. Luca

107. Kai

108. Kayden

109. Vincent

110. Bentley

111. Robert

112. Jude

113. Brandon

114. Bryce

115. Emmett

116. Everett

117. Jonah

118. Jake

119. Wesley

120. Finn

121. Ben

122. Weston

123. Silas

124. Jameson

125. Bennett

126. Santiago

127. Leonardo

128. George

129. Charles

130. Theodore

131. Damian

132. Kaiden

133. Maddox

134. Sam

135. Xander

136. Brantley

137. Riley

138. Hayden

139. Jax

140. Theo

141. Aidan

142. Jayce

143. Maxwell

144. Marcus

145. Graham

146. Colin

147. Ashton

148. Abel

149. Kingston

150. Braxton

151. Caden

152. Ryker

153. Calvin

154. Bryson

155. Kaden

156. Kyle

157. Malachi

158. Kaleb

159. Patrick

160. Angel

161. King

162. Nicolas

163. Avery

164. Bradley

165. Giovanni

166. Miguel

167. Eric

168. Kevin

169. Dean

170. Preston

171. Aj

172. Omar

173. Antonio

174. Sean

175. Elliott

176. Ali

177. Diego

178. Ezekiel

179. Justin

180. Brady

181. Grant

182. Matteo

183. Ivan

184. Axel

185. Lorenzo

186. Arthur

187. Joel

188. Juan

189. Maverick

190. Elliot

191. Enzo

192. Jose

193. Rowan

194. Luis

195. Beau

196. Cayden

197. Zane

198. Jaden

199. Jase

200. Oscar

Chapter 5:
The 200 Most Popular Girl's Names

This chapter contains a list of the 200 most popular girl's names for 2016.

1. Emma

2. Olivia

3. Sophia

4. Ava

5. Mia

6. Isabella

7. Charlotte

8. Amelia

9. Harper

10. Emily

11. Madison

12. Abigail

13. Avery

14. Lily

15. Ella

16. Sofia

17. Chloe

18. Evelyn

19. Aria

20. Scarlett

21. Aubrey

22. Ellie

23. Zoey

24. Zoe

25. Addison

26. Elizabeth

27. Grace

28. Hannah

29. Audrey

30. Riley

31. Layla

32. Mila

33. Victoria

34. Nora

35. Natalie

36. Penelope

37. Lucy

38. Lillian

39. Brooklyn

40. Savannah

41. Claire

42. Anna

43. Violet

44. Leah

45. Stella

46. Maya

47. Alice

48. Skylar

49. Maria

50. Samantha

51. Sarah

52. Eva

53. Sadie

54. Sophie

55. Kennedy

56. Hazel

57. Madelyn

58. Hailey

59. Julia

60. Gabriella

61. Aaliyah

62. Mackenzie

63. Paisley

64. Eleanor

65. Peyton

66. Caroline

67. Bella

68. Kylie

69. Piper

70. Ariana

71. Clara

72. Cora

73. Arianna

74. Kaylee

75. Taylor

76. Camila

77. Isabelle

78. Autumn

79. Quinn

80. Annabelle

81. Alyssa

82. Alexa

83. Aurora

84. Emilia

85. Lydia

86. Ruby

87. Valentina

88. Naomi

89. Isla

90. Allison

91. Elena

92. Alexis

93. Gianna

94. Madeline

95. Luna

96. Eliana

97. Hadley

98. Aubree

99. Lilly

100. Sydney

101. Reagan

102. Vivian

103. Bailey

104. Serenity

105. Kayla

106. Rylee

107. Faith

108. Willow

109. Nevaeh

110. Ivy

111. Sara

112. Alexandra

113. Isabel

114. Brielle

115. Molly

116. Kinsley

117. Lyla

118. Morgan

119. Liliana

120. London

121. Jade

122. Adalyn

123. Paige

124. Lauren

125. Everly

126. Natalia

127. Delilah

128. Emery

129. Brooke

130. Ana

131. Jasmine

132. Adeline

133. Khloe

134. Melody

135. Gracie

136. Kate

137. Arya

138. Jordyn

139. Norah

140. Eden

141. Melanie

142. Adalynn

143. Athena

144. Charlie

145. Abby

146. Mya

147. Laila

148. Maggie

149. Elise

150. Jocelyn

151. Reese

152. Eliza

153. Katherine

154. Sienna

155. Rose

156. Josephine

157. Brianna

158. Makayla

159. Mary

160. Kendall

161. Andrea

162. Lola

163. Payton

164. Nur

165. Lila

166. Mckenzie

167. Ariel

168. Juliana

169. Alaina

170. Callie

171. Gabrielle

172. Hayden

173. Cecilia

174. Adelyn

175. Trinity

176. Emerson

177. Genesis

178. Nicole

179. Evie

180. Alana

181. Arabella

182. Laura

183. Leilani

184. Alina

185. Lucia

186. Genevieve

187. Tessa

188. Nina

189. Presley

190. Keira

191. Alexandria

192. Teagan

193. Summer

194. Kaitlyn

195. Leila

196. Fiona

197. Juliette

198. Anastasia

199. Josie

200. Alayna

Chapter 6: Unique Names for Boys and Girls

Names from locations

One of the hottest trends in names for boys and girls especially in the United States is the practice of naming the baby after a country, place, landmark, or town.

Since most of the places' names don't have any implications attached to them as to whether they are meant for a boy's name or a girl's, parents usually choose a name that can be both be used for a girl or boy. Some of the names include:

Clyde – a river in Scotland

Fraser – Town in France

Jordan – country in the Middle East

Paris – capital of France

Maine – one of the 50 states in the US

France – a country in Western Europe

Kailash – a Himalayan mountain

Acton – town in Britain

Louvain – city in Belgium

Sidney – City in Australia

Kerry – county in Ireland

Daryl – area in France

Nevada – western US state

Names of Historical References

This can be a famous historical site or an important historical event your ancestors have become a big part of. It is a good possibility that any name that reflect pride in country and family will be given as names for your children.

Machias – found in Maine

Sturbridge – found in the city of Massachusetts

Montpelier – in Vermont

Lexington

Walden

Concord

Parker

Names from the Bible

Parents who consider themselves as religious will always turn to the Bible for name inspiration for their children. Some would also pick names of patron saints and even angels.

Boy's Names

Andrew – Disciple of Jesus

Like – Apostle

Stephen – a martyr

Jason – colleague of Paul

Joseph – father of Jesus

Jairus – leader of the synagogue

Alexander – son of the man who carried Jesus' cross

James – brother of Jesus

Timothy – disciple of Paul

Girl's Names

Anna – a prophetess

Julia – woman greeted by the apostle Paul

Mary – Mother of Jesus

Bethany – a village in the book of Luke

Eunice – mother of Timothy

Magdala – town of Mary Magdalene

Hoebe – woman in the book of Romans

Salome – mother of John the Apostle

Names of Angels

Gabriel – guardian angel of fire

Michael – guardian angel of the threshold

Tubiel – guardian angel of summer

Zadkiel – guardian angel of benevolence

Attarib – guardian angel of winter

There are also those names from different cultural traditions. One perfect example are Scandinavian names that are indeed distinctive. Some of the popular names include:

Boy's Names

Anders

Bjørn

Gustaf

Per

Karl

Dag

Oskar

Rolf

Jens

Olaf

Lars

Nil

Girl's Names

Astrid

Britta

Dagmar

Eva

Grete

Ingrid

Siane

Ulta

Kari

Anna

Heide

Margareta

Elisabeth

Native American Names

Chaska – first son

Len – meaning flute

Pezi – grass

Galegina – male deer

Nashoba – wolf

Diwali - bowl

Hohots – bear

Sani – old

Zotom – one who bites

Girl's Names

Chapa – Beaver

Kaya – older sister

Opa – owl

Sahkyo – mink

Inola – black fox

Taima – fox

Natane – daughter

Acadia – village

Eyota – great

Zitkala – bird

<u>Hindu Names</u>

Boy's Names

Amar

Anand

Kala

Kesin

Pramod

Vadin

Krishna

Adri

Balin

Valin

Vasin

Vinod

Rohin

Hardeep

Dalal

Girl's Names

Anala

Deva

Chandi

Kalinda

Lalita

Natesa

Rudra

Sita

Veda

Greek Mythological Figures

You very well know your Greek mythology back in your high school days, don't you? Naming your kids after a Greek god is not a bad idea at all. Greek gods and goddesses have been considered the recipient of some of the best names you can encounter.

Here are some of the Greek gods and goddesses and a little bit something about them:

Male Gods - Inspirational Names for Boys

Adonis – God of beauty

Res – God of war

Orion – God of the hunt

Pan – God of the shepherds

Triton – God of the sea

Apollo – God of war

Eros – God of love

Hermes – Messenger of the gods

Pontus – God of the sea

Zeus – King of the gods

Atlas – held the world on his shoulders

Helios – God of the sun

Female Gods - Inspirational Names for Girls

Artemis – Goddess of nature

Athena – Goddess of wisdom

Eris – Goddess of debate

Aphrodite – Goddess of beauty

Hestia – Goddess of the home

Nike – Goddess of victory

Selena – Goddess of the moon

Persephone – goddess of the spring and rebirth

Iris – Goddess of the rainbow

Demeter – Goddess of the Earth

Roman Mythological Names

Just like their Greek counterparts, the Roman gods and other mythological figures have also became influential in shaping parents' present day thoughts. They have provided parents' names for their babies. Some of the common baby names that you can choose from for your little gods and goddesses include:

Inspirational Names for Boys

Hercules – Jove's son

Sol – God of the sun

Mars – God of war

Romulus – founder of Rome

Jupiter – God of all

Cupid – God of love

Janus – God of doorways

Mercury – messenger of the gods

Saturn – God of harvests

Ulysses – King of Ithaca

Vulcan – God of fire

Inspirational Names for Girls

Ceres – Goddess of farming

Diana – Goddess of the moon

Luna – Goddess of the moon

Pomona – Goddess of fruit tress

Vesta – Goddess of the home

Aurora- Goddess of the sunrise

Minerva – Goddess of wisdom

Terra – Goddess of the earth

Victoria – Goddess of Victory

Flora- Goddess of the flowers

Latona – Mother of Dianna and Apollo

Chapter 7:
Famous Names

Popular Names from Politicians and Influential People

Some people like to name their children after presidents and influential people.

So if you are passionate about politics, this list may help narrow down your choices. Nothing grand here. Remember, plain works. Feel free to use a variation of the names as well, these are just here to give you a few more ideas!

Names of Presidents for Boys

George Washington

James Monroe

William Henry

James Garfield

Franklin Pierce

John Adams

James Madison

Theodore Roosevelt

Calvin Coolidge

James Buchanan

Andrew Johnson

Ulysses Grant

John Quincy Adams

Thomas Jefferson

Martin Van Buren

John Tyler

Zachary Taylor

Millard Fillmore

Rutherford Hayes

Chester Arthur

James Polk

William McKinley

William Taft

Benjamin Harrison

Warren Harding

Ronald Reagan

Bill Clinton

George Bush

Barack Obama

Other Notable Politicians

Moon Landrieu – Secretary of Housing and Urban Development

Oveta Culp Hobby – Secretary of Health, Education and Welfare

Alben Barkely – Vice President under Harry Truman

Schuyler Colfax – Vice President under Ulysses Grant

Danfort Quayle – Vice President under George Bush

Famous Names of Writers and Artists

If you adore Shakespeare, Agatha Christie, and Maya Angelou among others, you might consider naming your child after one of the people listed below.

Boy's Names

Gabriel Garcia

Herman Merville

Nathaniel Hawthorne

Walt Whitman

Gustave Klimt

David Hockney

Geoffrey Chaucer

Salvador Dali

Girl's Names

Alice Walker

Agatha Christie

Frida Kahlo

Georgia O' Keeffe

Jane Austen

Nora Ephron

Gloria Steinem

Famous Rock and Roll Names

Boy's Names

Elton Johjn

Freddie Mercury

Jimmy Buffett

John Lennon

Paul McCartney

Robert Palmer

David Lee Roth

Kurt Cobain

Bruce Springsteen

Girl's Names

Alanis Morrissett

Annie Lennox

Janis Joplin

Tina Turner

Melissa Etheridge

Alison Moyet

Popular Celebrity Names

Boy's Names

Andy Garcia

Antonio Banderas

Brad Pitt

Christopher Reeves

Dennis Quaid

Eddie Murphy

Clint Eastwood

Harry Hamlin

Dean Cain

Harvey Keitel

James Dean

Jimmy Stewart

Lenny Bruce

Macaulay Culkin

Ralph Maccio

Mel Gibson

Matt Dillon

Sammy Davis

Steven Segal

Wesley Snipes

William Baldwin

Girl's Names

Alicia Silverstone

Angela Bassett

Bette Davis Demi Moore

Glenn close

Goldie Hawn

Meryl steep

Michelle Pfeiffer

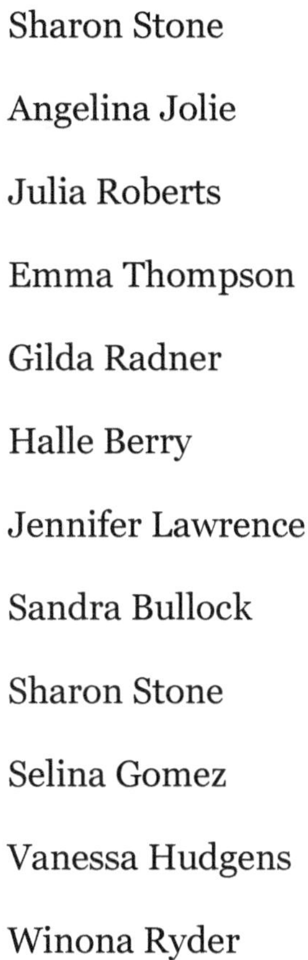

Sharon Stone

Angelina Jolie

Julia Roberts

Emma Thompson

Gilda Radner

Halle Berry

Jennifer Lawrence

Sandra Bullock

Sharon Stone

Selina Gomez

Vanessa Hudgens

Winona Ryder

What Famous Celebrities are Naming their Babies

Americans adore celebrities and this fact can't help but be mirrored in the names given to kids. Not only do parents name their kids after their Hollywood idols, they also go out of their way naming them after the kids that the stars are having.

For Girls

Claudia Rose – daughter of Michelle Pfeiffer

Zoe – daughter of Amanda Bearse

Sasha – daughter of Steven Spielberg

Annie – daughter of Jamie Lee Curtis

Molly – daughter of Terri Garr

Tara – daughter of Oliver Stone

Danielle – daughter of Jerry Lewis

Renee – daughter of Rod Stewart

Matalin Mary – daughter of Mary Matalin

For Boys

Nicolas – son of Jean-Claude Van Damme

Jett – son of Jon Travolta

Cody – son of Robin Williams

Jack Henry - son of Meg Ryan

Alexander James - son of Andy Mill

Christian Aurelia - son of Arnold Schwarzenegger

Michael Garrett – son of Melissa Gilbert

Famous Country Music Names

Country music is a big hit. This is precisely the reason why many parents would love to have their babies named after their favorite country music singer.

Boy's names

Chet Atkins

Garth Brooks

George Jones

Kenny Rogers

Waylon Jennings

Lee Clayton

Girl's Names

Crystal Gayle

Loretta Lynn

Taylor Swift

Shania Twain

Wynonna Judd

Dolly Parton

Naomi Judd

Reba McEntire

Patty Lovelace

Chapter 8:
Bonus Names For Boys

For Boys

<u>A</u>

Adi – A Hindu name meaning beginning

Akil – intelligent

Abiel – God is my father

Ace – unity

Acestes – A mythological Trojan king

Achelous – God of the river

Achiya – God is my brother

Adar – ruler or prince

Adin – a Hebrew word meaning attractive

Adler – an eagle

Adom – God's blessing

Aedus – An Irish word meaning fire

Aidan – warm

Ainmire – Great lord

Akela – Hawaiian word for lucky

Akilesh – King of all

Akshay – forever

Ala – superior

Alipate – bright

Altair – bird

Amariah – God has spoken

Amycus – friendly

Andor – Eagle

Ansel – one who follows

Apara – achild that comes and goes

Apia – God is my father

Arach – prepared

Arcas – from the Greek word meaning the son of Jupiter and Callisto

Arles – promise

Arrio – fierce

Arshad – devoted

Arundel – valley of the eagle

Aryeh – lion

Atiah – ready

Audric – noble ruler

Auriel – lion of God

Avi – My God

Aviram – My father is string

Ayize – let it come

Azi –youth

Aziz – powerful

Azriel – God is my help

B

Balraj - strong king

Baram - son of the people

Baron – warrior

Baruch – blessed

Baism – smile

Bem – an African word meaning peace

Benes – blessed

Benjiro – peaceful

Berdy – very smart

Beval – like the wind

Bhanu - the sun

Boleslaw – Great glory

Bond – man of the land

Boone – good

Borivoj – great soldier

Botan – long life

Boure – county

Borr – youth

Bour – rock

Bozydar – a gift of God

Brand – firebrand

Brock – badger

Bron – origin

Bryson – nobleman's son

Bruke – fortress dweller

<u>C</u>

Cadby – soldier's estate

Caelan – powerful warrior

Calder – brook

Camey – champion

Can – a Vietnamese word for advice

Carlin – little champion

Carthach – loving

Casimir – one who brings peace

Cephas – rock

Chal – boy

Chane – plant

Chetzron – walled town

Chim – bird

Chonen – gracious

Cid – rooster

Coiseam – stable

Coman – noble

Connor – much desire

Conroy – wise man

Cort – courageous

Coyle – soldier

Creighton – rocky area

Cuinn – wisdom

Curran – hero

Cyril – lord

<u>D</u>

Dag – day

Daivat – powerful

Daly – to gather together

Damon – gentle one

Dang – valuable

Dar – pearl

Dasan – chief

Deems – child of a judge

Deker – to pierce

Devin – poet

Dhaval – white

Din – calm

Dishi – virtuous man

Donovan – dark

Doron – gift from God

Doyle – black stranger

Duriel – God is my home

Dyzek – He who loves the earth

E

Eallair – steward, one who lives in a monastery

Eamon – rich protector

Eben – stone

Enam – gift from God

Ennis – only choice

Epena – stone

Eran – observant

Erel – I see the Lord

Ettore – loyal

Eyulf – lucky wolf

Ezer – help

F

Fadi – to save

Fahim – intelligent

Falak – a Hindu word meaning heaven

Faxon – long hair

Fidel – faith

Finlay – fair hero

Firoz – winner

Folant – strong

Frobe – wise

<u>G</u>

Gage – pledge

Garek – wealth

Gautier – powerful leader

Gaurav – pride

Genty – snow

Gerwyn – fair love

Giannis – God is good

Gifford – brave, provider

Gilam – joy of the people

Gillean – a good servant

Gillie – song

Gipsy – wanderer

Godwin – good friend

Grady – famous

Gulzar – blooming

Gus – majestic

Gwynedd – blessed

<u>H</u>

Hadley – meadow of heather

Hakan – fiery

Halsten – rock and stone

Hamal – lamb

Hamiloton – fortified castle

Hanan – God is good

Hani – happy

Hannes – God is good

Hardwin – brave friend

Harish – Lord

Harkin – dark red

Harmon – Army man

Harshad – One who gives joy

Haskel – wisdom

Hawley – meadow with hedges

Heddwyn – blessed peace

Hemen – wolf

Heneli – ruler at home

Herleif – beloved army

Hideo – superb

Hillel – a Hebrew word meaning highly praised

Hitoshi – A Japanese word meaning first

Hod – wonderful

Hogan – youth

Holt – forest

Hoshama – a Hebrew word meaning God hears you

Huang - a Chinese word meaning wealthy

Hung – a Vietnamese word meaning courageous

Hy – hope

Hywel – famous

I

Iago – an Italian word meaning he who grabs by the heel

Ichiro – A Japanese word meaning first son

Ikaia – a Hawaiian word meaning God is my savior

Ilias – God is my God

Imrich – Strength at home

Iokia – God heals

Iram – shining

Irving – sea friend

Isi – a Japanese word meaning rock

Ives – yew wood

Iye smoke

<u>J</u>

Jabin – God has created

Jaidev – God of victory

Jayant – victorious

Jehan – God is good

Jeriah – God sees

Jesse – God exists

Jie – A Chinese word meaning wonderful person

Joab – praise the Lord

Jurgen – farmer

K

Kabir – A Hindu word meaning spiritual leader

Kaemon – right handed

Kahana – priest

Karel – man

Kaul – trustworthy

Kavi – poet

Keaton – hawk's nest

Keegan – passionate

Keitaro – blessed

Kelii – wealthy

Keo – God will increase

Keon – well born

Kidd – young

Kimo – to seize

Kinnard – top of the hill

Kiril – the Lord

Kirkwell – Church spring

Kiyoshi – A Japanese word meaning silent

Kliment – gentle

Koren – shining

Kwan – powerful

L

Lal – lovely

Lang – tall

Langley – long meadow

Lei – A Chinese word meaning thunder

Leith – broad river

Leor – I have light

Li – a Chinese word meaning strength

Lono – God of farming

Lucan – light

Ludomir – famous people

Ludvik – famous

Lyle – island

Lynden – hill with lime tress

M

Manley – Man's meadow

Mansoor – victor

Manu – second son

Manville – good town

Marid – defiant, bld

Marley – meadow near a lake

Maro – a Japanese word meaning myself

Marwood – lake in a forest

Mather – mighty army

Maui – God who discovered fire

Mercer – shop keeper

Merlin – falcon

Merrill – bright as the sea

Methodios – fellow traveler

Milo – generous

Minco – chief

Minh – brilliant

Moran – guide

Morven – big mountain peak

Munchin – little monk

<u>N</u>

Nadir - pledge

Naija – next born

Nandan – happiness

Natane – gift

Nero – strong

Netaniah – gift of God

Nhean – all-seeing

Nigan – in the lead

Nikolao – winning people

Noahdiah – meeting with God

Nuren – brilliance

Nye – honor

<u>O</u>

Oberon – noble

Odion – first born

Oistin – respected

Olery – leader

Oran – green

Oron – light

Osman – God protects

Osred – divine adviser

Oved – worshipper

Ozni – to listen

P

Pagiel – worships God

Palmer – one who carries palm branches

Parlan – farmer

Pascal – Easter child

Patwin – man

Penley – fenced meadow

Perkin – little Peter

Philemon – kiss

Pillan – highest essence

Pio – pious

Pitt – ditch

Ponce – fifth

Pramod – joy

Premm – love

Prescott – Priest's cottage

Pryderi – concern

Q

Qabil –able

Qued – decorated robe

Quigley – messy hair

Quincy – the fifth son

Quinnlan – strong man

Qirin – magic spell

Quon – bright

R

Raby – famous and bright

Radcliff – red cliff

Radek – famous ruler

Radman – joy

Radnor – red shore

Radoslaw – glory for God

Radwan – delight

Rafa = cure

Ragnar – warrior of judgement

Rahman – compassionate

Rajesh – king of kings

Raleigh – deer meadow

Ranier – mighty army

Rav – sun god

Rayhan – favored by God

Raza – content

Reece – fiery

Renor – to awaken

Renfred – string peace

Rhydderch – reddish brown

Rida – satisfied

Rimon – pomegranate

Roark – mighty

Rockwell – well of the rocks

Rohin - striving

Roka – wave

Romney – curving river

Rostislav – grabs glory

Rousse – red-haired

Rumford – to cross a wie river

Rycroft – field of rye

<u>S</u>

Saad – assistance

Saeed – happy

Sahen – flacon

Sahn – comparable

Saxon – leader

Seanan – old and wise

Sedgwick – sword place

Seldon – willow valley

Sereno – calm

Shafan – rabbit

Shafiq – sympathy

Shalmai – peace

Shamir – flint

Sheng – victory

Shomer – guardian

Shoval – road

Sikai – God is gracious

Siarl – man

Sigbjorn – victory bear

Simidh – supplanter

Siraj – light

Stancliff – stony cliff

Stein – stone

Sudas – good helper

Sveinn – strong youth

T

Tab – brilliant

Tahir – pure

Tal – rain

Tam – eight

Tank – god of the sky

Tas - bird's nest

Tavi – good

Tawfiq – good luck

Terrill – follower of thorn

Thabiti – a man

Thane – landlord

Thanos – royal

Theron – hunter

Thorndike – throny riverbank

Thu – autumn

Thurlw – thor's hill

Tilon – hill

Toa - brave

Toril – attitude

Tyson – fireband

Tzevi – deer

U

Udell – yew grove

Ugo – intellect

Ulf – wolf

Umed – desire

Urien – privileged birth

Useni – tell me

Uttam – best

Uziah – God is my strength

V

Valentine – strong

Van – appearance

Varden – green mountains

Varil – water

Varun – God is water

Vidor – happy

Vijay – victory

Vinod – fun

Vito – alive

Von – hope

Vui – cheerful

<u>W</u>

Wail – one who returns to Allah

Walden – forested valley

Walid – newborn

Waller – wall maker

Walton – walled town

Wardell – watchman's hill

Ware – observant

Warford – river crossing by the weir

Wen – born in winter

Weston – western town

Whitby – farm with white walls

Whitfield – white field.

Wit – life

Wunand – God is good

Wycliff – wHite cliff

<u>X</u>

Xanthus – blonde

Xayvion – new house

Xenos – guest

Xing-fu – happiness

<u>Y</u>

Yair – God will teach

Yaphet – attractive

Yarb – herb

Yardley – enclosed meadow

Yash – famous

Ye – a Chinese word meaning universe

Yemon – guardian

York – yew tree

Yuval – brook

Yves – yew wood

Z

Zahavi – gold

Zahur – flower

Zan – well-fed

Zbigniew – get rid of anger

Ze'ev – wolf

Zelimir – desires peace

Zephyrus – west wind

Zerem – stream

Zevid - present

Zitomer – to live in fame

Ziven – lively

Zotom – one who bites

Zwi – gazelle

Zygmunt – victorious protection

Chapter 9:
Bonus Names For Girls

For Girls

<u>A</u>

Aba – born on Thursday

Abelia – sigh

Abia – great

Abiah – God is my father

Adah – decoration

Adeleke – brings happiness

Adila – just

Adonia – beauty

Adya – Sunday

Afra – color of the earth

Afua – born on Friday

Ahalya – beautiful

Ai – a Japanese word meaning love

Aine – joyous

Aisha – life

Ajalaa – earth

Akamai – a Hawaiian word meaning pure

Akhila – total

Akilina – eagle

Akiva – shelter

Ala – fragrant

Alani – orange

Alcestis – heroine

Aleka – noble

Aleta – little winged one

Alida – wing

Alisi – noble

Allya – to rise

Almera – refined woman

Alohi – bright

Am – the moon

Amadi – celebration

Amaui – bird

Amee – nectar of life

Amitola – rainbow

Amoli – valuable

Anais – gracious

Anci – grace of God

Anina – answered prayer

Ardelle – enthusiastic

Arub – affectionate

Asisya – juice of God

Asoka – flower

Auina – slope

Ayla – oak tree

Ayelet – deer

Ayondela – bending tree

Azhar – flower

Azza – gazelle

B

Banan – fingertips

Bara – a Hebrew word meaning to choose

Bariah – to succeed

Basilia – royal

Bechira – to select

Bel – apple wood

Belita – little beauty

Berit – brilliant

Bevin – singer

Bibiane – lively

Bina – knowledge

Blanchefleur – white flower

Bryn – mountain

Bunny – good

C

Cainwen – blessed fair one

Cala – fortress

Calantha – flower

Caltha – yellow flower

Candace – royalty. This is a title used by Ethiopian queens.

Cari – gentle stream

Carys – loved

Cedrica – gift

Chandani – moonlight

Chantou – flower

Charmaine – song

Charu – attractive

Chasina – strong

Chinue – blessings of God

Chloe – young blade of grass

Chumina – God

Clelia – glorious

Corvina – raven

Cyrilla – godly

<u>D</u>

Dai – a Japanese word meaning grand

Dalit – running water

Danae – a mythological figure in Greek mythology

Danuta – given by God

Darda – pearl of wisdom

Delicia – delight

Deonaid – God is gracious

Devasha – honey

Dhavala – white, pure

Dielle – God

Dilys – faithful

Dobra – no war

Donata – given

Dore – ornate

Dorit – generation

Douce – sweet girl

Dumia – quiet

Dyvette – arrow's bow

E

Eadoin – friendly

Earlene – leader

Edmee – to love

Eiddwen – blessed

Eirian – silver

Ekela – noble

Elama – God's people

Elberta – shining, noble

Eldreda – counselor

Elele – messenger

Eliana – God has answered prayers

Elined – idol

Elita – chosen one

Ellice - noble

Elrica - leader of all

Eme – beloved

Emera – industrious

Enid – life

Enfys – rainbow

Erina – speech

Esmeralda – Emerald

Etenia – rich

Etta – diminutive

Evania – serene

Ezrela – God is my strength

F

Fadila – virtue

Faline – catlike

Fang – fragrant

Fariha – happy

Fayza – winner

Fedora – gift from God

Fiala – violet

Filippina – lover of horses

Fisi – blossom

Fola – honorable

Frigg – beloved

Fuyu – a Japanese word meaning winter

<u>G</u>

Gaia – earth

Galya – god has redeemed

Ganesa – Goddess of wisdom

Gefjun – She who gives wealth

Genna – small bird

Geona – glorification

Ghada – graceful

Gitel – good

Gleda – happy

Glenys – holy

Greer – observant

Guida – guide

Gunn – battle

Gurice – lion cub

H

Hadi – calm, serene

Hania – resting place

Hanita – grace

Harita – wind

Haru – born in spring

Hasanati – good

Hasika – laughter

Haukea – A Hawaiian word for snow

Hauma – gentle

Hayat – alive

Hebe – goddess of youth

Hedy – wonderful

Helia – sun

Helmine – protector

Herlindis – gentle army

Heulwen – sunshine

Hialeah – beautiful posture

Hillani – carried by heaven

Hiral – brilliant

Honovi – powerful

Hoolana – happy

Hua – a Chinese word meaning flower

Hue – old fashioned

Huynh – color yellow

I

Idony – Goddess of Soring

Idra – fig tree

Ife – love

Ilana – tree

Imara – firm

Imana – God of all

Imogen – innocent

Ines – pure

Iola – worthy god

Iseult – ruler of the ice

Ishana – desire

Itiah – God is here

Iulaua – good talker

Iwilla – I will rise

<u>J</u>

Jade – Jade stone

Jael – mountain goat

Jaha – pride

Jaira – God teaches

Jalila – great

Jamelia – good looking

Janan – spirited

Jerusha – married

Jethra – plenty

Jezebel – virginal

Jocasta – happy

Jodi – praised

Jonina – dove

Johna – God is good

Jora – autumn rain

Juh – flower

Jumana – born on Sunday

K

Kaarina – pure

Kaci – He commands peace

Kadenza – with rhythm

Kai – forgiveness

Kakalina – pure

Kalana – flat land

Kalaudia – lame

Kalauka – famous

Kalika – flower pod

Kalila – beloved

Kalilea – pillow talk

Kalindi – river

Kalinn – stream

Kalita - famous

Kalola – woman

Kalyan – beautiful

Kamari – like the moon

Kame – tortoise

Kamea – sole one

Kameli – honey

Kaminari – thunder

Kanani – beautiful

Kanda – magic

Kanestie – guide

Kani – sound

Kanjana – God of love

Kanti – lovely

Kanya – daughter

Kapua oo flower

Karima – noble

Karmle – garden of grapes

Karmil – red

Karuna – compassion

Kasi – holy city

Kasmira – bringing peace

Kataniya – small

Kauila – acclaimed woman

Kaveri – river

Kaena – fire

Keiki – child

Kela – second child

Kelekea – garden flower

Kenisha – beautiful woman

Keohi – woman

Kerensa – love

Ketzia – tree bark

Khalida – forever

Kichi – lucky

Kimaya – Godlike

Kimimela – butterfly

Kineta – dynamic

Kini – God is good

Kinsey – family

Kiran – light

Kiska – pure

Kiwa – born on the border

Konia – talent

Kuali – queen

Kumari – daughter

Kumi – braid

Kuri – chestnut

Kwabina – born on Tuesday

Kylie – boomerang

Kyoko – mirror

Kyri – dark

L

Lahela – lamb

Laka – docile

Lareina – queen

Lark – brid

Latavia – pleasant

Laudomia – praise the house

Leah – slowly but surely

Leala – loyal

Leanda – lion

Leeba – heart

Lehua – sacred

Leiko – proud

Leinana – beautiful

Leisi – lace

Lenis – smooth, silky

Lerato – love

Leslie – low meadow

Levina – lightning

Levona – Frankincense

Li – a Chinese word meaning pretty

Libena – love

Licha – nobility

Linden – tree

Linit – relax

Liona – roaring lion

Liviya – lioness

Lois – famous soldier

Lokalia – garland of roses

Lola – sorrow

Loni – ready for battle

Losa – rosa

Lucita – light

Lujayn – silver

Lulani – heaven's peak

Lusela – bear foot

M

Maata – lady

Machi – ten thousand

Madhu – honey

Madra – mother

Maemi – honest smile

Maeve – delicate

Magena – new moon

Maha – big eyes

Mahaska – white cloud

Mahira – quick

Mai – flower

Maikai – good

Maima – gold

Maisie – pearl

Maka – earth

Makani – wind

Makawee – abundant

Mala – garden

Malama – sunshine

Malia – defiance

Malie – lucky

Malina – peaceful

Malkin – battle maiden

Maluhi – peaceful

Malva – delicate

Manal – accomplished

Mandara - tree

Mani – prayer

Mansi – picked flower

Manuela – God is among us

Marabel - beautiful

Maraea – sea woman

Maratina – warlike

Mardi – Tuesday

Margie – direction

Marina – from the sea

Marisol – bitter sun

Marjani – coral

Masa – direct

Masela – warlike

Matelita – powerful warrior

Mausi – picking flowers

Mavis – thrush

Maysa – walk proudly

Mazal – fate

Meara – jolly

Meda – prophet

Medora – gift from Mother

Meena – fish

Mehal – rain

Mehli – a Hindu word meaning rain

Meiron a- lamb

Melcia – ambitious

Melia – yellow

Meliora – better

Melita – honey

Melody – song

Melosa – sweet

Mema – hardworking

Mena – strength

Merav – to increase

Mercedes – mercy

Meredith – great leader

Meri – ocean

Meriel – brilliant seas

Meriwa – thorn

Merry – happy

Mesha – ram

Mesi – water

Migina – new moon

Mi-hi – lovely joy

Miki –family tree

Milcah – adviser

Minal – fruit

Mineko – peak

Minowa – moving voice

Mirabel – wonderful

Miri – mine

Misae – white sun

Misao – A Japanese word meaning loyal

Miyo – beautiful generation

Mizuko – water child

Moani – light breeze

Moemu – two bears

Moneka – earth

Monifa – I am lucky

Montana – mountain

Mora – blueberry

Morela – apricot

Morna – tender

Mosi – first born

Muna – desire

Musidora – gift from the muses

Muteteli – dainty

My – pretty

Myrddin – fortress by the sea

Mystique – mysterious

Myung – hee – smart

<u>N</u>

Nada – dew at sunrise

Nagida – wealthy

Magisa – beach

Nahla – drink

Naia – dolphin

Nailaha – one who succeeds

Navit – beautiful

Neala – champion

Nechama – comfort

Neda – born on Sunday

Nedaviah – God is charitable

Neem a- born during good times

Nehanda – strong

Nell – light

Neola – young girl

Nerida – sea nymph

Niamh – bright

Nili – this is a Hebrew acronym for "The glory of Israel will not repent"

Bonus Names For Girls

Nima – tree

Niobe – fern

Nitsa – shining girl

Nola – white shoulder

Nudar – golden

Nuru – daylight

Nyla – winner

Nyura – grace

O

Ocin – rose

Odessa – long journey

Ofa – love

Ohela – tent

Ola – protector of men

Oleda – noble

Oliana – flowering green

Olvyen – white footprint

Oma – leader

Ona – grace

Ondine – little wave

Oneida – anticipation

Oni – desired

Oona – unity

Orange – orange fruit

Orflaith – golden lady

Ornice – pine tree

Orsa – female bear

Oseye – happy one

Otzara – wealth

Owena – well born

Ozera - help

P

Padma – lotus

Palila – bird

Plama – palm

Pamela – honey

Pandita – scholar

Parvin – star

Patia – leaf

Pausha – month in the Hindu year

Pedzi – last child

Pelipa – lover of horses

Penelope – bobbin weaver

Peni – His mind

Pepita – God will add

Perdita - lost

Pilar – pillar

Piper – bagpipe player

Pita – fourth daughter

Q

Questa – hunter

Quintina – fifth

Quiterie – peaceful

R

Rabiah – breeze

Radhiya – agreeable

Radomira – famous, happy

Rafya – God heals

Raya – friend

Raziya – agreeable

Rehema – compassion

Rekha – line

Rena – melody

Rin – park

Rohana – sandalwood

Roniya – Joy of God

Rosamond – famous protector

Roselani – heavenly rose

Roula – defiant

Ruri – emerald

Ryba – fish

<u>S</u>

Sabina – A Roman clan's name

Sada – virgin

Sadira – lotus tree

Sagara – ocean

Saidah – happy

Sakari – sweet one

Salihah – virtuous

Salima – safe

Salus – goddess of health

Samina – happy

Sananda – joy

Sandeep – enlightened

Santana – saint

Santavana – hope

Saril – running water

Sasha – protector of men

Seda – forest echo

Seini – God is gracious

Sela – princess

Shada - - pelican

Shahira – famous

Shameena – beautiful

Shanasa – wish

Shea - request

Sherika – Easterner

Shilra – lovely

Shimona – to listen

Shina – loyal

Shizu – quiet

Shu – a Chinese word meaning tender

Sofronia – wise

Sook – purity

Sorcha – clear

Starling – bird

Sula – large bird

Sushanti – silence

Sylvia – from the forest

T

Tacey – quiet

Tahira – pure

Tain – new moon

Takara – treasure

Talal – dew

Talise – beautiful water

Talya – lamb

Tamah – marvel

Tamanna – want

Tami – people

Tanvi – young woman

Taree – tree branch

Tertia – third

Tevy – angel

U

Udiya – fire of God

Urbi – princess

Ushi – ox

Uwimana – daughter of God

<u>V</u>

Vanda - - Variation of Wanda

Vani – voice

Varsha – rain shower

Vera – faith

Verdad – truth

Verena – true

Verity – truth

Vespera – evening star

Vigilia – alert

Vinh – gulf

Vorsilla – little she – bear

W

Wafa – faithful

Walentya – healthy

Warda – protector

Washi – eagle

Whitley - white field

Wilona – desire

Wisdom – wisdom

Wren – bird

Wyome – big field

<u>X</u>

Xanthe – yellow

Xiang – fragrant

Xuan – spring

<u>Y</u>

Yachi – good luck

Yaki – spring

Yamina – ethical

Yanaha – she confronts an enemy

Yashila – successful

Yashna – prayer

Yelena – light

Ypa – snow maiden

Yoi – born in the evening

Yon – rabbit

Yoshino – fertile land

Yusra – rich

Yusra – rich

Z

Zahara – shine

Zahra – blossom

Zahreh – happiness

Zalika – well born

Zaneta – God is gracious

Zea – grain

Zel – cymbal

Zho – Character

Zilpah – dignity

Zina – hospitable

Zinnia – flower

Zippora – little bird

Zirah – coliseum

Zita – seeker

Zora – dawn

Zubaida – marigold

Zulema – peace

Zuzela – wife of a bull

Zytka – rose

Conclusion

Thanks again for taking the time to pick up this book!

You should now have a lot of baby names to choose from! I hope you found this book to be helpful and enjoyable!

If you enjoyed this book, please take the time to leave me a review on Amazon. I appreciate your honest feedback, and it really helps me to continue producing high quality books.